PANDAS!

A MY INCREDIBLE WORLD PICTURE BOOK

MY INCREDIBLE WORLD

Copyright © 2023, My Incredible World

All rights reserved. This book or any portion thereof may not be reproduced or used in any manner whatsoever without the express written permission of the copyright holder.

www.myincredibleworld.com

Pandas are black and white bears native to the bamboo forests of China.

Pandas are also known as **Giant Pandas**.

They can grow up to 6 feet (1.8 m) tall and weigh up to 300 pounds (136 kg)!

Pandas are **omnivorous**, eating mostly bamboo, but also some fish and small animals.

They can eat as much as 40 pounds (18 kg) of bamboo per day!

Pandas have super strong jaws that help them crush bamboo.

They have a special bone in their wrist (a **pseudo-thumb**) that helps them grip their food!

Pandas are solitary animals, only coming together to mate and share food.

While rare, a group of pandas is called an **embarrassment**!

Female pandas are called **sows**, while males are **boars**.

Baby pandas are called **cubs**.

Panda cubs are born pink and hairless!

They weigh only 4 ounces (113 grams) at birth!

Pandas are excellent climbers and can easily climb trees and steep hillsides.

They also love to play and have been seen sliding down snowy hills on their bellies!

Pandas are great at rolling and doing somersaults!

They are known to do this to avoid predators.

Pandas have a great sense of smell, which helps them find food.

They also have amazing hearing and can detect sounds that humans can't hear!

Pandas communicate with each other through a variety of vocalizations.

They bark, growl, squeak, and make a sheep-like bleating noise!

Pandas are incredible!